This book
belongs to:

........................................................

Published in Great Britain by Brimax,
An imprint of Autumn Publishing Group

Published in the US in 2004 by Byeway Books Inc,
Lenexa KS 66219 Tel 866.4BYEWAY

www.byewaybooks.com

© 2004 Autumn Publishing Group

Printed in China

# Pixie Pup
# is naughty

Pixie Pup likes hiding his bones in secret places where they will never be found by hungry 'bone hunters'! The trouble is, Pixie Pup always forgets where he has hidden them!

One day, after his afternoon nap, Pixie decided it was time for a chew on the big, juicy bone that he had hidden in a safe place.

First he looked under the table. But it wasn't there.

I'm sure I hid my bone here! thought the playful pup. Where else could it be?

Perhaps Pixie had left his bone on top of the table? Holding the edge of the tablecloth in his teeth, Pixie gave it a hard tug.

WHOOSH! The tablecloth flew off the table – and landed on Pixie Pup! Peering out from beneath the tablecloth, Pixie looked around.

"Well, I guess my bone wasn't on top of the table, after all!" he sighed. "I wonder where else I could have put it?"

Pixie was being very naughty!

Maybe Pixie had hidden his bone outside? Yes, that's where it would be!

When he was sure that no one was watching, Pixie crept out of the door and padded down the path.

After sniffing along the ground for ages, the naughty pup stopped near the shed. Then as fast as he could, he dug a hole.

Soon, the pup's paws were covered in sticky mud! But he still hadn't found his big, juicy bone!

So Pixie's bone wasn't under the table, it wasn't on top of the table – and it wasn't buried outside.

"My bone must still be indoors!" woofed the pup, racing back along the path.

Leaping on to the sofa, Pixie sniffed and scratched at the cushions – and then sniffed and scratched some more. But he couldn't find his big, juicy bone!

What a muddy mess naughty Pixie left on the sofa and cushions!

Pixie tried to think where he had last seen his bone. It wasn't under the table, or on top of it. It wasn't outside – and it wasn't on the sofa. Could it be in the kitchen?

Pixie ran out of the living-room, down the hall and into the kitchen. He was in such a hurry he knocked over his bowl of water.

SPLASH! "Oops! What a mess I've made!" woofed Pixie, as water spilled over the kitchen floor. "And I still can't find my big, juicy bone!"

Bounding up the stairs, Pixie decided to search in the bedrooms.

"Ah, now I remember!" woofed the pup. "I'm sure I hid my bone behind these pillows!"

Leaping on to a bed, Pixie used his paws to push a pillow on to the floor. But his bone wasn't there!

Pixie sniffed around inside the pillowcase, then picked it up with his teeth and gave it a good shake. But all he found were a few floaty feathers that tickled his nose.

Poor Pixie! He had searched all over the house and outside, but he still couldn't find his big, juicy bone.

He stopped for a rest and sighed, "Those nasty bone hunters must have taken my bone! I'm really bored now and I need a bone to chew."

As he closed his eyes for a nap, Pixie tried hard to remember where he had last seen his bone. Suddenly, his eyes flew open. Now I remember! he thought, happily.

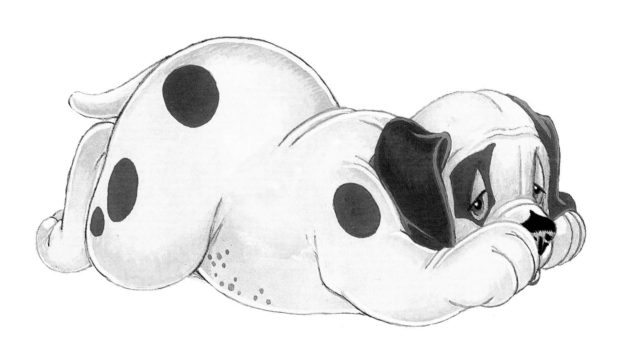

Pixie jumped to his feet, raced down the stairs, along the hallway – and into the kitchen.

Tucked away in a corner of the room was the pup's basket. "Woof! Woof! Woof!" he barked.

Pixie skidded across the kitchen floor, jumped into his basket and began to search under the blanket. With his nose twitching and tail wagging, the pup sniffed around.

The bone had to be there somewhere!

And it was! Picking up the big, juicy bone, Pixie happily trotted out of the kitchen, unaware of the muddy mess he had made that day.

"I must find a really good hiding place to bury my bone before those naughty bone-hunters find it!" woofed the playful pup.

At last, Pixie decided to bury his bone in a new secret place outside.

Oh, dear! It looks like the pup is going to make another muddy mess!

# Do you know?

1 What does Pixie like to hide?

2 Where did the pup first look for his big, juicy bone?

3 What flew off the table and on to the pup's head?

**4** Where did Pixie dig a hole?

**5** What did the pup knock over?

**6** Where did Pixie find his bone?

Answers: